Quick Expert
Ancient Egypt

Jill Laidlaw

Published 2009 by
A & C Black, an imprint of Bloomsbu[r]y
50 Bedford Square, London, WC1B [:]

www.bloomsbury.com

ISBN HB 978-1-4081-0856-7
PB 978-1-4081-1293-9

Series consultant: Gill Matthews

Text copyright © 2009 Jill Laidlaw

The right of Jill Laidlaw to be identified as the author of this work has been asserted by her in accordance with the Copyrights, Designs and Patents Act 1988.

A CIP catalogue for this book is available from the British Library.

Every effort has been made to trace copyright holders and to obtain their permission for use of copyright material. The authors and publishers would be pleased to rectify any error or omission in future editions.

This book is produced using paper that is made from wood grown in managed, sustainable forests. It is natural, renewable and recyclable. The logging and manufacturing processes conform to the environmental regulations of the country of origin.

Produced for A & C Black by Calcium.

Printed in China by C&C Offset Printing Co Ltd, Shenzhen, Guangdong

All the internet addresses given in this book were correct at the time of going to press. The author and publishers regret any inconvenience caused if addresses have changed or sites have ceased to exist, but can accept no responsibility for any such changes.

Acknowledgements
The publishers would like to thank the following for their kind permission to reproduce their photographs:
Cover: Shutterstock: Mirek Hejnicki, Maugli, Holger Mette, Dan Ionut Popescu.
Pages: Corbis: Bojan Brecelj 11t; Dreamstime: Wormold 13b; Istockphoto: Luke Daniek 6–7, Jeremy Mayes various pages, Manuel Velasco 14; Photolibrary: The Print Collector 19; Shutterstock: 10, Kharidehal Abhirama Ashwin 13t, Mario Bruno 17, Zhu Difeng 16, Pichugin Dmitry 7t, Iconex 8r, Vladimir Korostyshevskiy 21, Maugli 11b, Luciano Mortula 15, Juriah Mosin 18, Nagib 9, Jovan Nikolic 8b, David Peta 5b, Jose Antonio Sanchez 20, VanHart 12, Alena Yar 5t. Map: Geoff Ward 4.

10 9 8 7 6 5 4 3 2

Contents

Who Were the Egyptians?

Egypt is found in the north of Africa. It has the Mediterranean Sea on one side and the Red Sea on the other.

When was ancient Egypt?

About 7,000 years ago ancient Egypt was two separate kingdoms, one at each end of the River Nile. The River Nile flows from the south to the north. So, the south end was called Upper Egypt. The north end was called Lower Egypt.

About 2,000 years later, Upper Egypt conquered Lower Egypt. One king, called King Menes, ruled both kingdoms for the first time.

Did you know!

There were 365 days in an Egyptian year – just like our years – but they had ten days in a week!

This is a map of ancient Egypt, showing some of its many important sites.

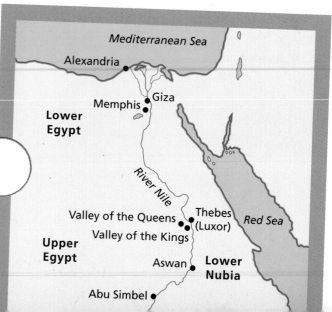

Mediterranean Sea
Alexandria
Giza
Memphis
Lower Egypt
River Nile
Valley of the Queens
Valley of the Kings
Thebes (Luxor)
Red Sea
Upper Egypt
Aswan
Lower Nubia
Abu Simbel

4

What did the Egyptians give to us?

The Egyptians gave us **pyramids** and hieroglyphics. Hieroglyphics are the oldest form of writing in the world. Hieroglyphics use pictures as words.

The Egyptians wrote about their history in hieroglyphics.

The pyramids are the oldest stone buildings in the world.

The River Nile

There were not many roads in ancient Egypt – the Nile was the main highway. Goods from other lands, such as food, and massive blocks of stone for building pyramids and **temples** were all carried in boats along the River Nile.

Farming

The Nile was the reason Egypt was so rich. The river flooded every year (mid-June to October) leaving rich, black mud, called silt, that was great for farming.

Water from the River Nile runs into canals cut into farmland. This waters the crops.

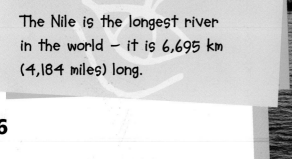

Did you know?

The Nile is the longest river in the world – it is 6,695 km (4,184 miles) long.

Food

Crops grown next to the Nile included barley, vegetables, wheat, grapes, beans, garlic, melons, and onions.

People braved crocodiles (who tried to eat them) and hippos (who tried to overturn their boats) to catch fish from the Nile.

The ancient Egyptians were afraid of hippos, but they also worshipped them.

Irrigation

Water from the Nile was used to feed the soil – the Egyptians built canals between their fields to carry the water to as much land as possible. This is called irrigation.

Trade and the Army

The River Nile was busy with **merchant** ships arriving from other countries and leaving for other ports.

Imports

The Egyptians bought gold, ivory, wood, and animal skins from people in other parts of Africa. They bought olive oil and silver from countries across the Mediterranean Sea and from the **Aegean Islands**.

Exports

The Egyptians sold goods such as **papyrus**, wine, **linen**, grain, metals, and precious stones.

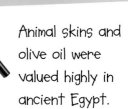

Animal skins and olive oil were valued highly in ancient Egypt.

8

Archers fired arrows from chariots, as well as on foot.

The army

There were times when the Egyptians did not have an army and there were other times when their army was large and powerful.

The Egyptian army had archers, foot soldiers, and **charioteers**. They also employed **mercenaries** to fight for them.

Foot soldiers did not have any armour to protect themselves – not even shoes. They carried just a simple bow and arrow, which they used in battle.

Did you know?

Soldiers grew their hair long to protect their heads – only the commanders had helmets.

Everyday Life

Most Egyptians worked as farmers. Children worked in the fields, too. When the fields were flooded, people worked for the **pharaoh** building temples, palaces, and pyramids.

Houses

Most people in ancient Egypt lived close to the River Nile. All houses were made out of bricks made from mud, baked hard in the sun.

Did you know?

Many men and women wore wigs, perfume, and make-up.

Curved blades, called sickles, were used to cut corn.

10

Schools

Most people could not read or write. They had to pay to go to school. Schools were mostly for boys, but girls from rich families were educated as well.

This wall painting shows an ancient Egyptian father with his children.

What they wore

Ancient Egypt, like Egypt today, was very hot so people did not wear many clothes. Children mostly ran around naked. Boys usually had shaved heads with a little ponytail on one side.

Barter

The Egyptians did not have money. People were paid in goods such as food. Then they swapped this for other things. This is called bartering.

Some women wore cones of perfumed fat on their heads.

Egyptian Gods

The ancient Egyptians had almost 2,000 gods. Egyptian gods were usually half-human and half-animal.

The myth of the sun god

Myths were told about the gods. The Egyptians believed that Re, the sun god, created the world. They thought that Re was reborn every day and sailed his boat across the sky. Re sailed through the **underworld** at night.

The Pharaoh Akhenaton worshipping Aten, the Lord of Heaven and Earth. Aten became an important god while Akhenaton was pharaoh.

Queen Nefertari (far right) is shown with the goddesses Maat (far left) and Isis (centre), and the god Horus in this painting.

Some gods...

- Horus looked after the pharaoh and had the head of a **falcon**.

- Hathor was the goddess of music, love, dancing, and happiness. She was married to Horus.

- Re was the sun god and had the head of a hawk.

- Osiris was the god of death and rebirth. He taught the Egyptians to farm.

- Isis was the great mother goddess and was married to Osiris – her brother!

- Anubis was the god of the dead, with the head of a **jackal**.

This wall carving is of Horus (left) and Hathor (right).

13

Temples

Ancient Egyptians worshipped some gods at small shrines (places to pray) they made in their homes.

The biggest and most important gods were worshipped in grand temples. Ordinary people were only allowed to go a little way into the temple. Only priests and the pharaoh could go into the inner temple.

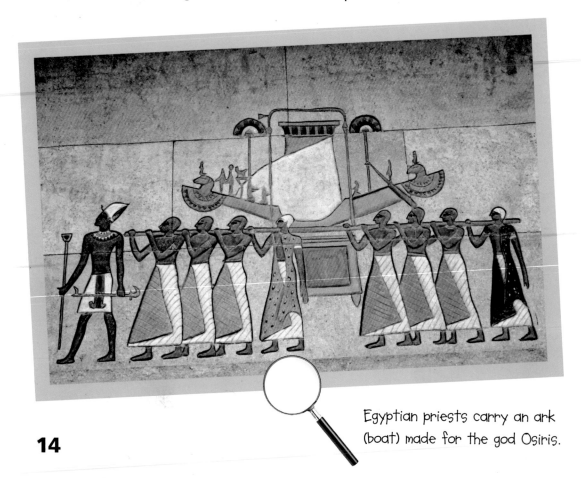

Egyptian priests carry an ark (boat) made for the god Osiris.

The Temple of Pharaoh Ramses II at Abu Simbel was carved from rock 3,300 years ago.

Temples

The Egyptians thought the gods made the first ever temple, so all temples were built to the same plan.

Each temple was dedicated to a different god and had a large statue of him. There was also a statue of the ruling pharaoh.

Many temples were built along the east bank of the River Nile, so that the sun would rise on them every morning.

Priests

Three times a day the priests:

-  said prayers to the god
- washed and dressed the statue of the god
- 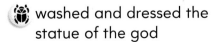 brought the statue food

Did you know?

Every day the priests washed in sacred temple water and shaved their whole bodies.

Pharaohs

The word "pharaoh" meant "great house" to the ancient Egyptians. They believed the spirit of the gods lived in the body of the pharaoh on Earth. They also thought that the pharaoh himself was a god. He made all the decisions and everyone had to obey him. He had two **viziers** to help him.

Dynasties

Egyptian history is divided up into periods of time called "dynasties" – this is how long each pharaoh's family ruled for.

Headdress

This pharaoh's headdress has a **cobra's** head. The cobra was thought to protect the pharaoh.

16

Queens

Pharaohs had one main wife and lots of other wives as well. Not many people were important enough to marry a pharaoh, so he sometimes married his own sister!

Did you know?

Tutankhamun is one of the most famous pharaohs. He came to the throne at the age of nine and died when he was 19 or 20 – some people think that he was murdered.

This is Queen Nefertiti, wife of Pharaoh Akhenaton.

Mummies

Egyptians believed that after death their spirit made a journey to the "next world", or underworld. After the spirit had been judged by the god Osiris, it would return to its body. This meant that Egyptians believed it was important to keep dead bodies "fresh" by making them into mummies.

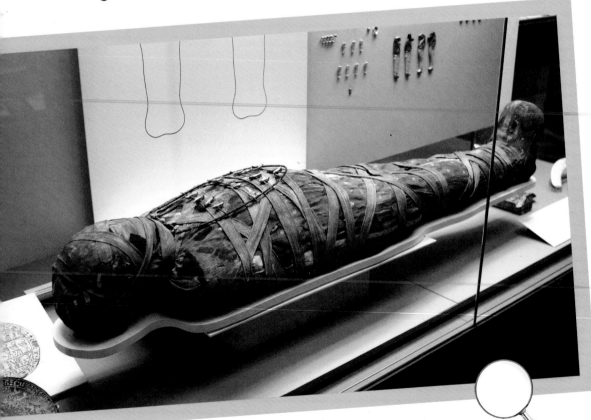

It took about 70 days to mummify a dead body.

Organs were put in **Canopic jars** such as these.

Making mummies

🪲 Wash the dead body.

🪲 Pull the **organs** out through a cut made in the side of the body. Store in jars.

🪲 Pull the brain out of the skull (by poking a hook up the person's nose) then throw it away.

🪲 Cover the body in a salt-like powder, called **natron**, and leave it for about 40 days.

🪲 Stuff the body with linen and sawdust soaked in oils.

🪲 Sew up the cut in the side.

🪲 Wrap the mummy in up to 20 layers of linen.

🪲 Place it in its coffin and put a mask over its head and face.

Pyramids

Important or rich people were mummified and buried in massive tombs called pyramids.

How were they built?

Nobody really knows how the pyramids were built. As far as we know, the Egyptians did not have machines to help them.

Teams of builders, masons, and workers chipped the blocks of stone for the pyramids out of the ground. Boats were used to transport the blocks along the River Nile. A single block could weigh as much as a car.

The biggest pyramid in Egypt is the Great Pyramid, built for Pharaoh Khufu. Its base is the size of eight football pitches.

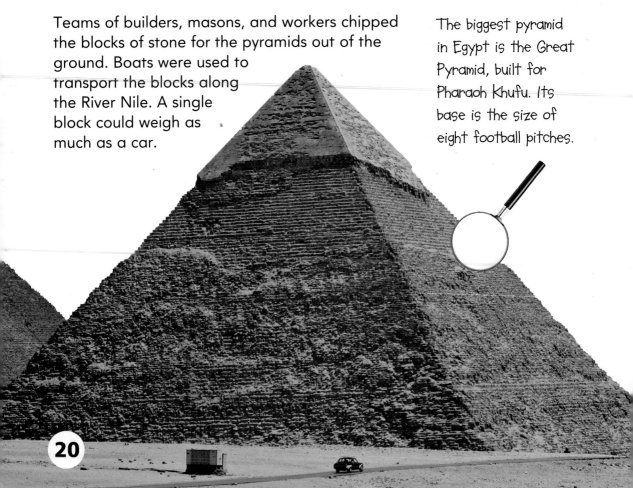

What's inside?

There was a burial chamber right in the middle of the pyramid. This was for the coffin.

Everything the person would need for the next world, such as food, wine, clothes, chariots, horses, pets, and furniture would be put in the pyramid.

The walls of pyramids were often painted with stories of the dead person's life, magic spells, and pictures of the gods.

21

Glossary

Aegean Islands a group of islands close to, and belonging to, Greece

Canopic jars jars for keeping important organs from a dead body safe. Each body usually had four of these jars

charioteers men who drive chariots

cobra a poisonous snake

falcon a type of hunting bird

jackal a type of wild dog

linen a material in which the mummified bodies were wrapped

mercenaries professional soldiers from other countries

merchant a person who travels to buy and sell goods

myth an ancient story

natron a white/yellow mineral used to preserve dead bodies

organs important parts of the body such as the liver, lungs, and heart

papyrus a type of reed that was cut and pressed into sheets to form a type of writing paper

pharaoh the name given to an Egyptian king

pyramid a tomb, shaped like a triangle on four sides, with a perfectly square base

temples places in which gods and goddesses are worshipped

underworld the place Egyptians believed they went after death. The underworld was ruled by Osiris

viziers the pharaoh's most trusted advisors. They helped him to run the country

Further Information

Websites

A summary of some of the things the ancient Egyptians invented can be seen at:
www.open2.net/whattheancients/egyptians.html

Nile facts, both ancient and modern, can be found at:
www.ancient-egypt-online.com/river-nile-facts.html

This British Museum site allows you to read stories about a day in the life of an ordinary family and a day in the life of an Egyptian nobleman.
www.ancientegypt.co.uk.menu.html

This British Museum site features pictures of the major gods and you can click onto the story of the first god.
www.ancientegypt.co.uk/gods/explore/main.html

Take a virtual tour through the tomb of Tutankhamun at:
www.kingtutone.com

Books

Ancient Egypt (Arts and Crafts of the Ancient World). Franklin Watts (2007).

Men, Women and Children in Ancient Egypt. Wayland (2008).

The Egyptians (Footsteps). Franklin Watts (2007).

Ancient Egypt by Jane Shutter. Wayland (2008).

The Ancient Egyptians by Jane Shutter. Wayland (2008).

Index